Killer Disasters

EARTHQUAKES

DOREEN GONZALES

PowerKiDS press
New York

Published in 2013 by The Rosen Publishing Group, Inc.
29 East 21st Street, New York, NY 10010

First Edition

Editor: Amelie von Zumbusch
Book Design: Greg Tucker
Layout Design: Julio Gil

Photo Credits: Cover Darrenp/Shutterstock.com; p. 4 Daniel Caselli/AFP/Getty Images; p. 5 Dimitar Dilkoff/AFP/Getty Images; pp. 6–7 James Balog/Stone/Getty Images; p. 8 Soner Kilinc/AFP/Getty Images; p. 9 Daniel Garcia/AFP/Getty Images; p. 10 Spencer Platt/Getty Images; p. 11 arindambanerjee/Shutterstock.com; pp. 12–13 Nicholas Kamm/AFP/Getty Images; p. 14 Feng Li/Getty Images; p. 15 Teh Eng Koon/AFP/Getty Images; p. 16 American Stock/Archive Photos/Getty Images; p. 17 Jim Richardson/National Geographic/Getty Images; p. 18 Scott Barbour/Getty Images; p. 19 NYPL/Science Resource/Photo Researchers/Getty Images; p. 20 Desiree Martin/AFP/Getty Images; pp. 21 (top, bottom) Russell Curtis/Photo Researchers/Getty Images; p. 22 Justin Sullivan/Getty Images.

Library of Congress Cataloging-in-Publication Data

Gonzales, Doreen.
Earthquakes / by Doreen Gonzales.
p. cm. — (Killer disasters)
Includes index.
ISBN 978-1-4488-7442-2 (library binding) — ISBN 978-1-4488-7515-3 (pbk.) —
ISBN 978-1-4488-7589-4 (6-pack)
1. Earthquakes—Juvenile literature. I. Title.
QE521.3G64 2013
363.34'95—dc23

2012000768

Manufactured in the United States of America

CPSIA Compliance Information: Batch #B3S12PK: For Further Information contact Rosen Publishing, New York, New York at 1-800-237-9932

CONTENTS

Rocking and Rolling

Every so often, the ground rocks and rolls and shudders and shakes. This is an earthquake. Movements in Earth's top layer, or **crust**, cause earthquakes. The crust is broken into huge pieces of rock known as **plates**. The plates sit on **magma**, or rock that is so hot that it is liquid. The plates move around

This bridge outside of Santiago, Chile, collapsed when an earthquake struck the area on March 4, 2010.

These people are waiting in line for food in Ercis, Turkey, in the days after an earthquake hit. The quake destroyed the homes of thousands of people.

on the magma. Sometimes, they bump into each other. This makes the ground shake, creating an earthquake.

Earthquakes can be powerful forces. They can make buildings fall and set off huge ocean waves called **tsunamis**. Sadly, earthquakes can also be deadly.

WHICH FAULT?

Earthquakes happen at **faults**, or breaks in Earth's crust. Faults are often at places where two plates meet. The rocks along a fault push against each other and move. In a normal fault, the rock on one side drops down below the rock on the other side. At a reverse fault, the rock on one side is pushed up over the rock on the other. A strike-slip fault happens when the rocks on either side slide past each other sideways.

As the rocks move, they are sometimes pushed in ways that make them bend and break. The breaking sends vibrations through the ground, causing an earthquake.

The San Andreas Fault, in California, is where the North American plate meets the Pacific plate. It is a strike-slip fault.

THE RICHTER SCALE

Scientists use tools called **seismometers** to measure an earthquake's vibrations, or **seismic waves**. Seismometers can sense even very tiny movements in Earth's crust. When an earthquake happens, it sends seismic waves rippling out from it. Seismic waves are strongest in the spot the earthquake happened. This is the earthquake's **epicenter**.

These people are standing in the streets of Simav, Turkey, after a 5.9-magnitude earthquake hit the area on May 19, 2011.

An 8.8-magnitude earthquake pulled apart this road in Chile in 2010.

Seismometers help scientists determine an earthquake's strength, or **magnitude**. The earthquake is then rated with a number from the Richter scale.

People do not usually feel earthquakes that are rated less than 2.0 on the Richter scale. A strong earthquake has a magnitude of about 6.0. An 8.0-magnitude earthquake is huge.

HAITI IN RUINS

In 2010, a 7.0 earthquake struck the island country of Haiti. The quake shook apart thousands of houses. It brought down schools and hospitals.

During the next few days, **aftershocks** racked the area. An aftershock is a small earthquake that hits an area after a larger one has struck.

After the 2010 earthquake, many Haitians who had lost their homes had to live in refugee camps. Sicknesses, such as cholera, swept through the camps, killing yet more people.

This church in the Haitian capital, Port-au-Prince, was destroyed in the 2010 earthquake.

The earthquakes and aftershocks left thousands of people dead and thousands more hurt. At least a million people lost their homes.

Helping those in need became especially hard because the earthquake ruined communication systems. Even so, countries all around the world found ways to get help to Haiti.

Disaster in Haiti!

Date:	**January 12, 2010**
Magnitude:	**7.0**
Aftershocks rated above 4.0:	**59**
Buildings damaged or destroyed:	**403,176**

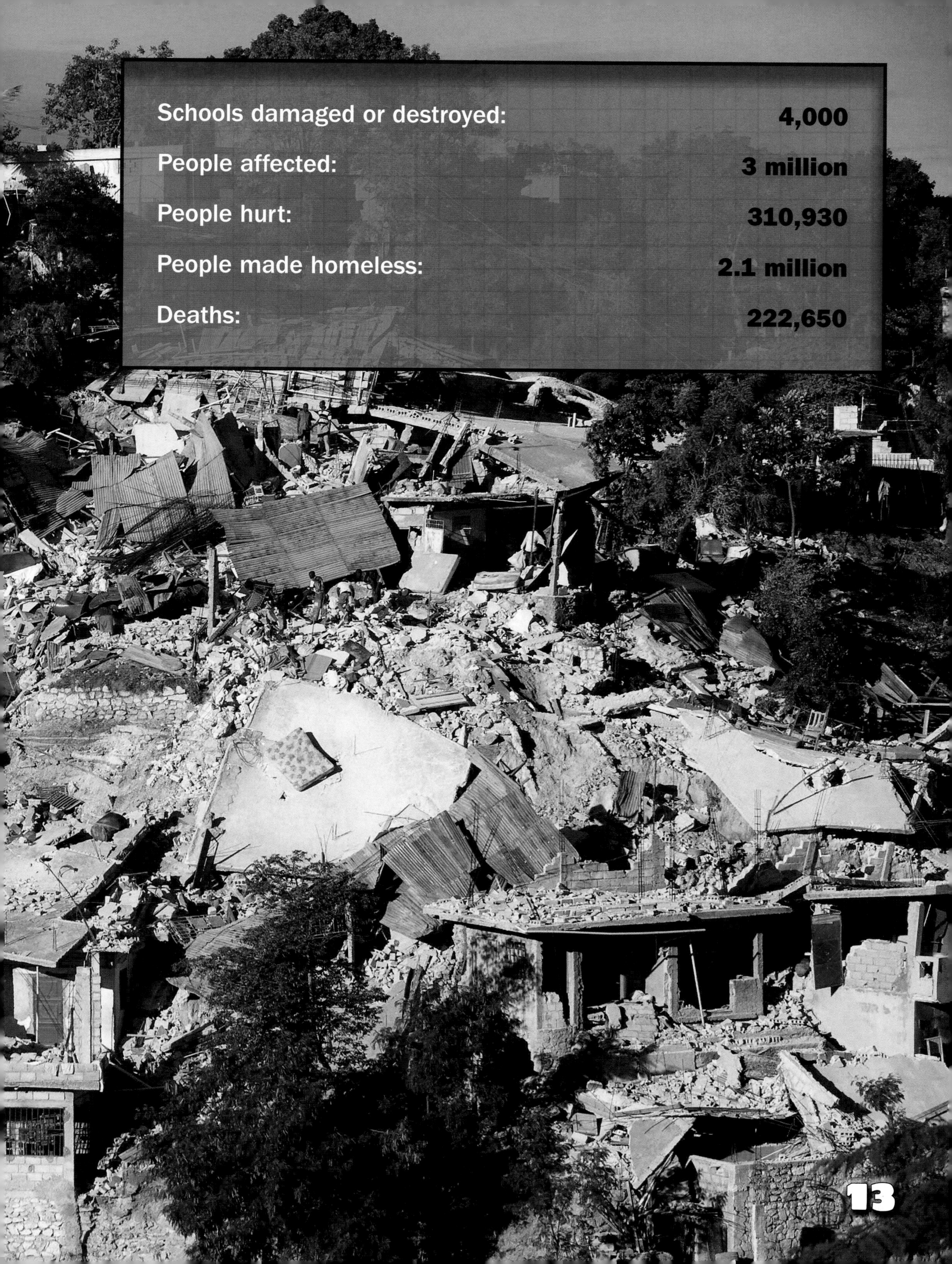

Schools damaged or destroyed:	4,000
People affected:	3 million
People hurt:	310,930
People made homeless:	2.1 million
Deaths:	222,650

CHINA QUAKE

In 2008, a 7.9-magnitude earthquake rocked the mountains of Sichuan, China. The earthquake was so strong it shook buildings more than 900 miles (1,448 km) from its epicenter.

Schools, hospitals, factories, and homes fell down. The earthquake

These girls are standing in the remains of their home after the 2008 earthquake in China destroyed it.

The 2008 earthquake in Sichuan, China, was one of the costliest natural disasters ever. It caused about $29 billion in damage.

broke water and gas pipes. Its shaking caused rocks to slide down mountains. The **landslides** ruined roads, buried buildings, and caused flooding. Aftershocks hit the area for months.

This was the worst earthquake to strike the area in 30 years. It left five million people without homes and more than 69,000 people dead.

CALIFORNIA'S FAULT

The San Andreas Fault runs for about 600 miles (970 km) along the coast of California. It can be seen in some places. The Pacific plate on the west side of the fault is slowly moving northwest. This makes the land along California's coast move about 2 inches (5 cm) each year.

The 1906 earthquake and the fire it caused destroyed more than 80 percent of San Francisco.

This house was damaged in the Loma Prieta earthquake. The earthquake occurred in California in 1989. Movement along the San Andreas Fault caused it.

The moving plates create small earthquakes in many places along the San Andreas Fault. In others, the strain builds up and causes major earthquakes. One of the deadliest earthquakes along the fault happened in 1906. That year, a 7.8 quake hit San Francisco. It started a huge fire and killed around 3,000 people.

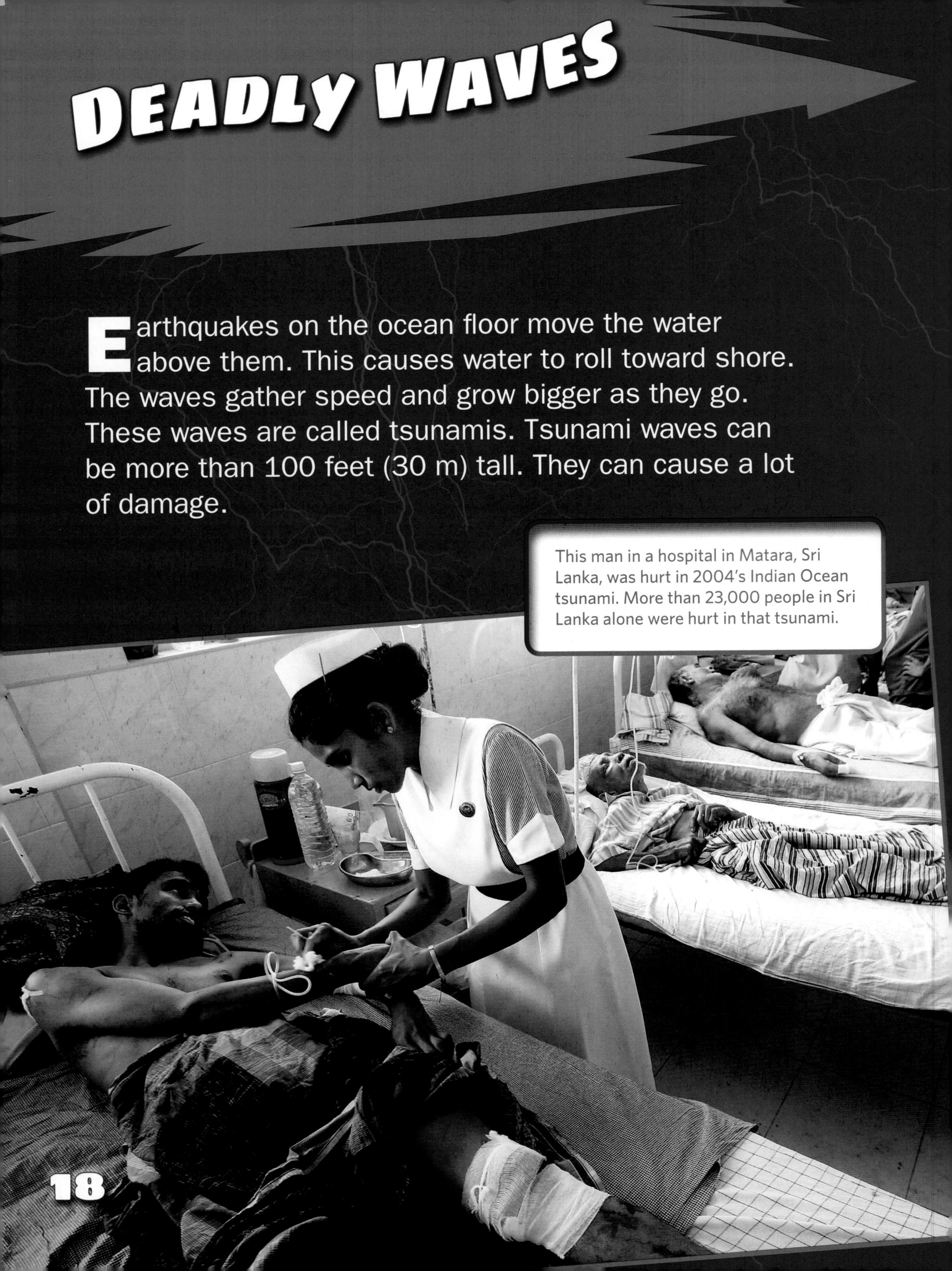

DEADLY WAVES

Earthquakes on the ocean floor move the water above them. This causes water to roll toward shore. The waves gather speed and grow bigger as they go. These waves are called tsunamis. Tsunami waves can be more than 100 feet (30 m) tall. They can cause a lot of damage.

This man in a hospital in Matara, Sri Lanka, was hurt in 2004's Indian Ocean tsunami. More than 23,000 people in Sri Lanka alone were hurt in that tsunami.

Here, you can see the same area on the Indonesian island of Sumatra both before the 2004 tsunami hit (top) and after (bottom).

In 2004, a 9.0 earthquake in the Indian Ocean moved the seafloor. This set off a huge tsunami that hit the coasts of many countries, traveling all the way to Africa. The tsunami did the most damage in Indonesia. By the time the ocean calmed, more than 200,000 people were dead.

LOOKING BELOW THE EARTH

Scientists study earthquakes to learn more about Earth. They also want to get better at knowing when an earthquake might happen.

Scientists do much of their work near faults. They drill deep into the ground and pull up pieces of rock from far underground. They study seismic waves to learn more about how movements in Earth's crust create

This scientist is recording movements in Earth's crust on Hierro, one of the Canary Islands. In 2011, a series of earthquakes hit the island.

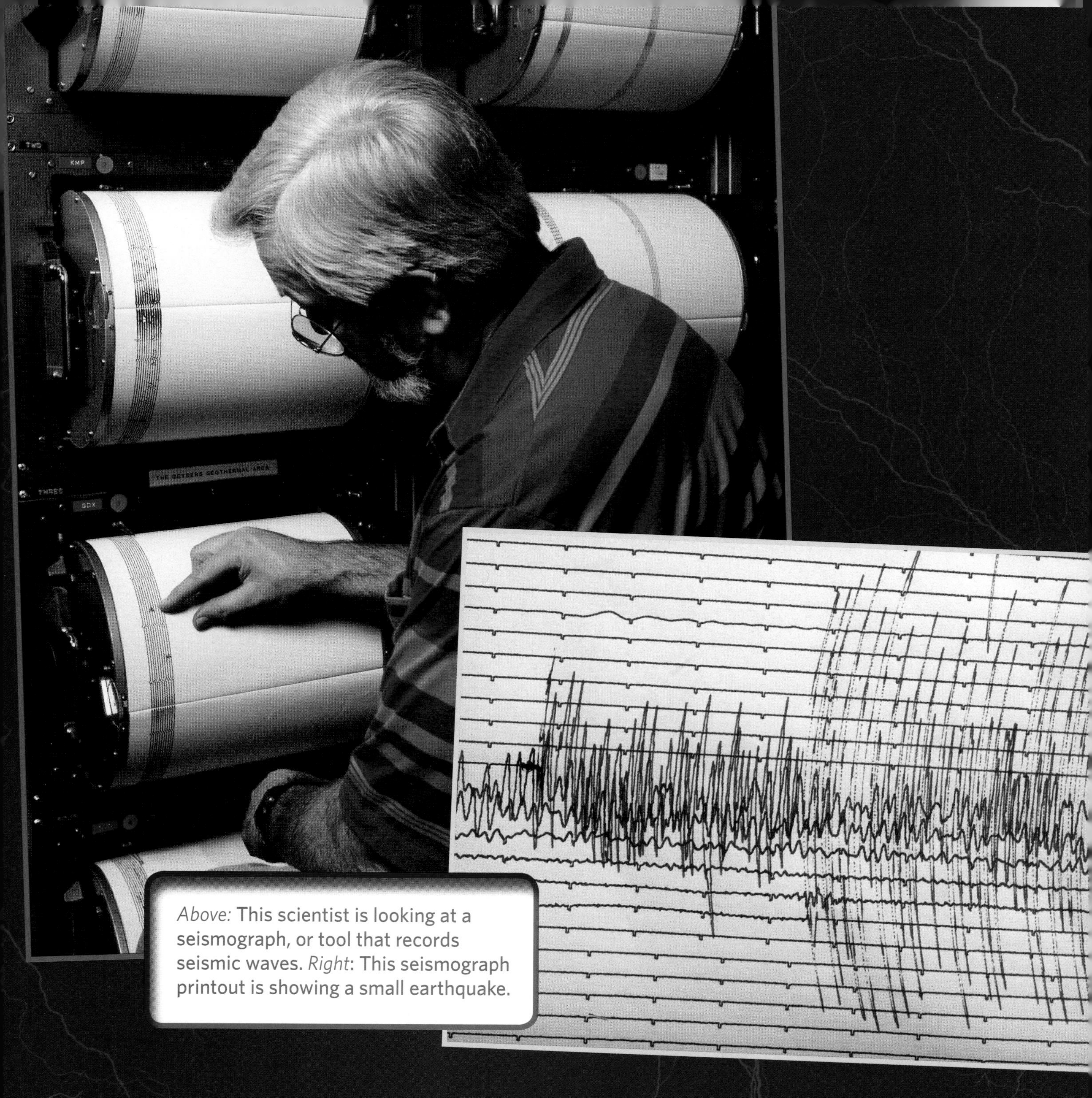

Above: This scientist is looking at a seismograph, or tool that records seismic waves. *Right*: This seismograph printout is showing a small earthquake.

earthquakes. Sometimes the waves warn scientists that a quake is coming.

Scientists use the information they gather to create **computer models** of earthquakes. These help them understand how earthquakes work and get better at knowing when one will strike.

Practice Being Safe

If you live in a place where earthquakes are common, keep an emergency kit on hand. It should include water and a battery-powered radio. If an earthquake hits, get under a table to stay safe from falling objects. Stay away from glass and do not go outside. If you are outside, move away from buildings and power lines.

Earthquakes can be dangerous. Practice what to do so you can keep yourself safe if one strikes.

These kids in San Francisco, California, are taking part in an earthquake drill. In this kind of drill, people practice what to do if an earthquake happens.

GLOSSARY

AFTERSHOCKS (AF-ter-shoks) Trembles in Earth's crust after an earthquake.

COMPUTER MODELS (kum-PYOO-ter MAH-dulz) Computer programs that show what might happen in real life.

CRUST (KRUST) The outside of a planet.

EPICENTER (EH-pih-sen-ter) The part of Earth's surface directly above the center of an earthquake.

FAULTS (FAWLTS) Cracks in Earth's crust, or outside.

LANDSLIDES (LAND-slydz) Movements of rock or earth down a slope.

MAGMA (MAG-muh) Hot, melted rock inside Earth.

MAGNITUDE (MAG-nih-tood) The measurement of something's strength.

PLATES (PLAYTS) The moving pieces of Earth's crust, the top layer of Earth.

SEISMIC WAVES (SYZ-mik WAYVZ) Waves caused by Earth's shaking.

SEISMOMETERS (syz-MAH-meh-terz) Tools used to measure the ground's movement.

TSUNAMIS (soo-NAH-meez) Series of waves that are often caused by movements in Earth's crust.

INDEX

WEBSITES

Due to the changing nature of Internet links, PowerKids Press has developed an online list of websites related to the subject of this book. This site is updated regularly. Please use this link to access the list: www.powerkidslinks.com/kd/quake/